Copyright © 2022 by Shalom Greenwald

All rights reserved. No part of this book, whole or in part, may be stored, reproduced, transmitted or translated in any form or by any means whatsoever, manually or electronically, without prior written permission from the copyright holder, except by a reviewer who wishes to quote brief passages in connection with a review written for inclusion in newspapers or magazines. The rights of the copyright holder will be strictly enforced.

Credits:
Illustrations by Sarah and Miriam Greenwald
Editing by Ian Grinblat of Crafted Expression

ISBN 978 0 64558 570 4

Every person is born with a natural curiosity. As we grow, our world expands and suddenly the potential is limitless. To consider the vastness and mostly unknown concept of outer space is to also recognize the Creator, an inspiring emotional and spiritual experience.

There are known global benefits for humankind to explore space besides encouraging international cooperation: satellites provide data on climate change, measure pollution, can be used to predict some natural disasters and help us protect our planet. There are constantly new scientific breakthroughs that challenge our assumptions and push our boundaries, a lesson for every area in our lives.

NASA also is a shining example of supporting others working towards the same goal. Every single day, they bring to life the acronym T.E.A.M. Together Everyone Achieves More.

This book about space exploration will delight every mind, tickle your imagination, and enhance your entire life. It is a must-read for every person ... on any planet.

Contents

Choose Your Own Adventure
1. Space Adventure — 1
2. Space Emergency — 5
3. Superstar Excursion — 10

Experiments
A. Balloon Rocket — 15
B. Balloon Powered Car — 16
C. Action and Reaction — 17
D. Film Canister Rocket — 18
E. Water Rocket — 19
F. Egg Dropping — 20
G. Baking Soda Rocket — 21
H. Self-Inflating Balloon — 22

The Planets of Our Solar System — 23

Jewish Education and Space Flight — 24

Space Adventure

Nathan was in a candy store eating every type of candy in all the colours of the rainbow - Red, Orange, Yellow, Green, Blue, Indigo and Violet.

He was feeling happy and carefree when suddenly, he was startled by a noise becoming louder and louder

BIP, BIP, BIIIP, BIIIP.

It was his alarm clock - the too-good-to-be-true candy store had been a dream.

Usually, Nathan would struggle to get up, but today was different. He woke in a heartbeat, jumped out of bed, ran to brush his teeth and get ready for school.

Today was a big day for Nathan, a day he had been waiting for as long as he could remember - the school excursion to the moon! Nathan was fascinated with all things related to outer space, the stars, the moon and the planets. He put on his best clothes and asked his self-driving car to take him to school as fast as possible. He could barely contain his excitement, so as soon as he reached his school, he ran to the classroom where Miss Ella was taking attendance. Every member of the class was present in the classroom because nobody wanted to miss this experience.

Miss Ella asked children to walk in an orderly fashion to the "Rocket Room" which was their spaceship. They found themselves in a circular classroom with windows - like a flying saucer - where Miss Ella told them all to take their seats and buckle up before she gave them instructions for the long journey. The children were just a bit disappointed when Miss Ella told them that they would be orbiting the moon but not landing as they were all too young for such a dangerous excursion.

– "Welcome aboard Flight EB07, the flying saucer service from Melbourne to the moon. We are currently first in line for take-off and expect to reach outer space ten minutes after blast-off and then it will take us twenty-four hours to arrive at the moon. Please fasten your seatbelts and secure all baggage in the overhead compartments. We also ask that your seats and table trays are in the upright position for blast-off. Please turn off all personal electronic devices, including laptops and mobile phones. Enjoy your spaceflight."

The rocket room began to rumble and rattle. Nathan was a bit afraid as this was his first time in a spaceship. Suddenly he felt a strong pressure as he closed his eyes and could feel the spaceship rising very quickly. Miss Ella explained to the children that the Earth's atmosphere has a series of layers, each with its own specific properties. Moving up from the earth's surface, these layers are named troposphere, stratosphere, mesosphere, thermosphere and finally the exosphere which gradually fades into the realm of interplanetary space.

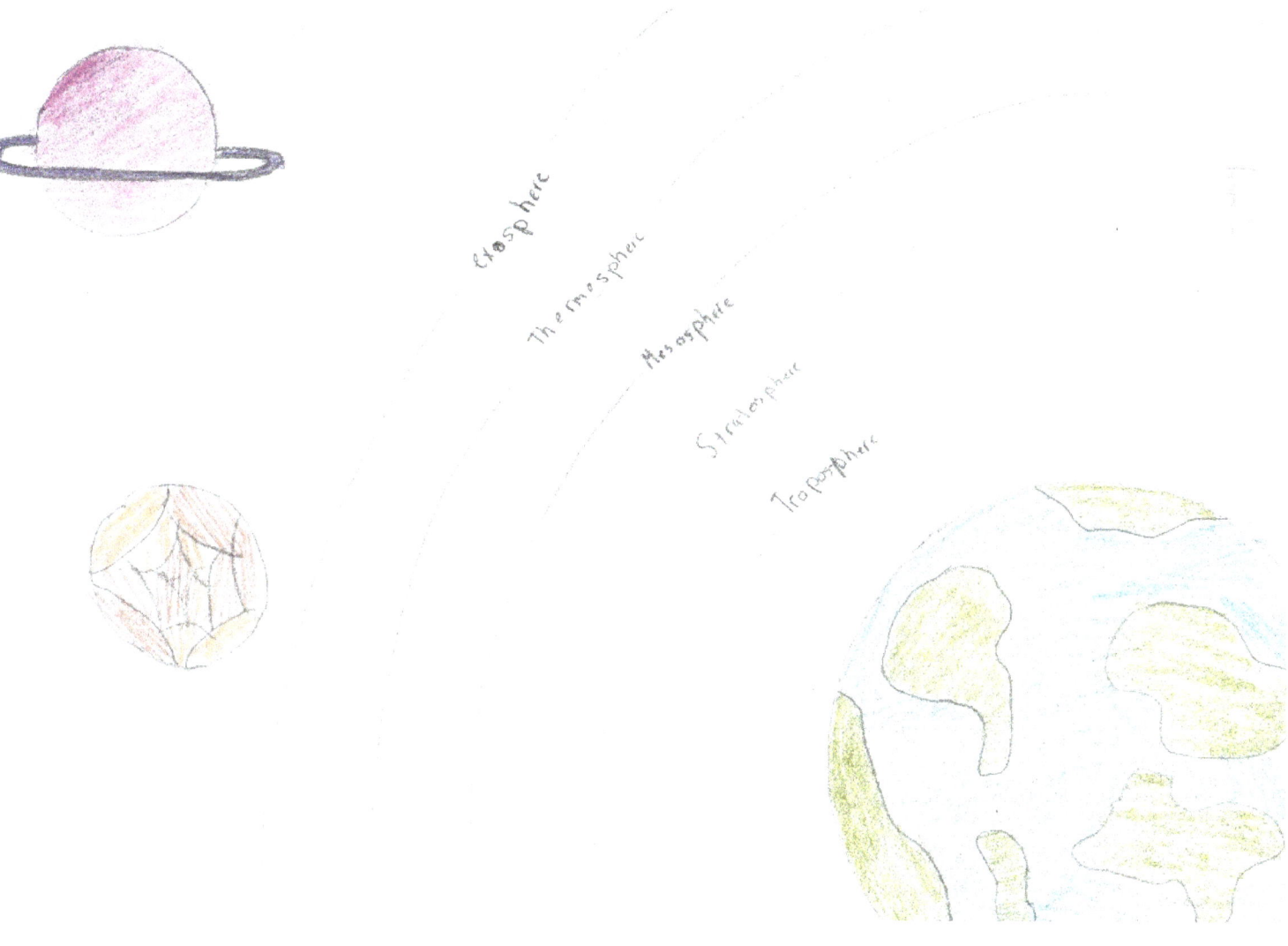

Nathan was scared to open his eyes, but when he heard other children exclaim "Wow, this is amazing!" and other children laugh, he became so curious that he finally opened his eyes and what he saw was indescribable - the Earth below looked like a huge blue shiny balloon and the countless stars were brighter than he could ever have imagined. After twenty-four hours of looking out at space the craft reached the moon, which they orbited twice before returning to earth.

Space Emergency

My name is Sarah, and I'm so excited today - I have my school bag, my lunch box and my water bottle ready for the space adventure with my teacher, Rivkah who told us she will be teaching us about space today.

The School bell is ringing. I must go to class. I'm so excited that I am tap dancing all the way to the classroom and towards my desk, but when I see my teacher is waiting, I stop dancing and I stand quietly by my desk.

Rivkah greets us, "Good morning, class" and we all respond, "Good morning" and take our seats. She draws pictures of planets on the board while talking about them. She tells us that Pluto is no longer classified as a planet - I was disappointed to hear that because I really like Pluto planet - it reminds me of the dog Pluto.

While my teacher is talking, I play with my Blu-Tack, forming it into a large button which I colour bright fire-engine red, using a red Texta.
Rivkah's voice fades as I press my red button and brace myself, "Here we go!"

The classroom turns into a spaceship, and our countdown begins:

9, 8, 7, 6, 5, 4, 3, 2, 1, BLAST OFF!

Our classroom rises through trees and is soon higher than any mountains as it passes through the clouds. I look up and, oh wow, I can see the planets and the stars! I point to a large striped planet and ask Rivkah what planet it is. She tells me it's Jupiter. Then she points out the Milky Way as our classroom approaches the moon. We pass low over its surface where I see a footprint in the dust. We are not the first ones here. Rivkah tells us that the moon always shines, no matter the circumstances - just as everyone in this world has a mission or purpose and must continue to shine in the world, no matter what anyone says, even in hard times, and we should never give up. Suddenly, the engine makes funny noises and our spacecraft stops.

- "Mayday! Mayday! We are stuck and have no way of getting back" Rivkah calls to Ground Control.
- "Press the red Emergency button," is the response from Ground Control.
- "I can't find the red button!" Rivkah calls in panic.

Rivkah asks us all to help her find the red Emergency button and I hold up the button I made – I think that if that button could send us into space, it must also work in an emergency.

- Oh! Thank you! Good girl, Sarah. As you have it in your hand, please quickly press the button!"

I push my big red emergency button. The spaceship rocks and descends really fast ....

I can feel the floor shaking as I hear Rivkah asking us what we thought about the space lesson. Of course - we all loved it! Rivkah is so pleased with us that she tells us there is no homework for tonight.
After school I tell my family all about my space adventure. I'm looking forward to tomorrow when we will learn about how a spaceship is built.

Have a good night. Now I must have my dinner. Toodles.

Superstar Excursion

Moishy was eating his way down a candy rainbow, along a road of red lollypops, yellow Laffy Taffy ropes, green peppermint sticks and blue bubble gum.

He skipped happily - there wasn't a cloud in the sky, the world was fantastic, nothing could upset him

- BIP BIP BIP -

Moishy's bedroom came into view as his eyes blinked open. It had all been just a dream!

He said Modeh Ani (short prayer recited upon waking), washed negel vasser (ritual washing of the fingers; Yiddish, nail water) and jumped out of bed. After that yummy dream, he was sure in the mood for some sugar cereal! After a hefty bowl of Fruity Pebbles, Moishy bentched (blessings after eating) and got ready for school. He was excited! Better than any candy-laden road was today's school trip... to the moon!

Moishy put on his best clothes, kissed his tzizis (fringed garment worn by Jewish males under their shirts) and almost flew out the door to school.

Morah (teacher) Chanah was already taking attendance.
- "Chaim?" "Here!"
- "Berel?" "Here!"
- "Yudi?" "Here!"
- "Ezra?" "Here!"
- "Moishy!" "Here, definitely, here!"
- "Well, then we're all set," Morah Chanah said. "Line up in an orderly fashion, please, kinderlach (children). Now is our chance to make a kiddish Hashem (bringing honor to God) in outer space!"

Moishy joined the line, his heart thumping, and followed his classmates to the circular-shaped Rocket Room. Inside, right in the middle of the room, glistened the sparkling white, spotlessly clean, spaceship. Morah Chanah instructed everyone to put on their space suits before they climbed aboard and buckled up.

"Welcome aboard Flight EB07, your direct service from Melbourne to the moon," the captain said gravely. "Please make sure that your baggage is secured in the overhead lockers and then fasten your seatbelts. We are currently first in line for take-off."

5, 4, 3, 2, 1... Blast off!

The boys held on to their yarmulkes (skullcaps worn by Jewish males).

"The moon is 386,400 kilometres away, so it will take three entire days just to get there", announced the Captain.
"Fortunately, we have all the yummy kosher (ritually fit for Jewish people to eat) food you could want!" Morah Chanah reassured her class.
Moishy remembered his delicious dream! Now it seemed to be coming true!

The space shuttle rumbled along through the air, speeding through the atmosphere, going faster and faster. For hours, the students played, sang, talked, slept and made a beautiful kiddish Hashem. Morah Chanah was so proud of them.
Then, as the third day approached, Moishy woke from yet another dream to the sounds of his classmates' excited squeals as they peeked out the window.

- "Wow!"
- "Would you look at that?!"
- "That's incredible!"

Moishy's eyes flew open, and his mouth dropped as he saw the moon looming ahead, its craters visible. Their spaceship was about to land. But then, looking upward through his window, he saw the most magnificent shiny blue ball. Planet Earth! Home!

After all that traveling, the class had only a short time to explore the moon - just a few hours - but they loved every second of it. They felt really inspired to think that they were the first group ever to have davened (Yiddish, meaning to recite the prescribed prayers) on the moon!

They returned to earth three days later, just in time for Shabbos (Sabbath, Day of Rest, Friday sunset until nightfall on Saturday), with a brand-new appreciation for the magnificent, endless universe Hashem (Hebrew substitute for the name of G-d) had created.

Experiments at Home

These experiments should only be attempted under adult supervision

1- Balloon Rockets

Aim: To teach children about thrust

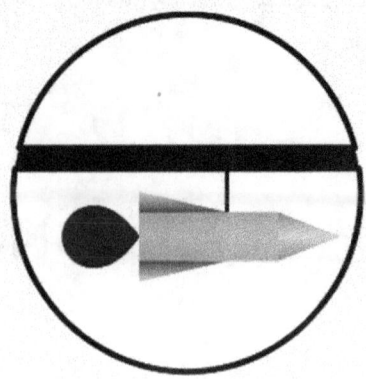

Materials required

1 x party balloon

Method

Blow into a balloon to inflate it until you cannot force in more air.
Let go of the balloon.
What happens?
Explanation: When you inflate the balloon, you are filling it with air, when you let go of the balloon, the air rushes out of the mouth of the balloon. As the air comes out of the balloon in one direction, it pushes the balloon in the opposite direction. This push is called thrust.
Does the balloon move in a straight line?

2 - Balloon Powered Car

Aim: To demonstrate the conservation of energy

Materials required

- 1 x square piece of cardboard (approx. 10 cm by 10 cm)
- 2 x straight straws
- 1 x bendy straw
- 2 x skewers
- 1 x party balloon
- 4 x plastic screw bottle lids
- 1 x sticky tape
- 1 x small rubber band
- 1 x pair of Scissors

Method

Using the sticky tape, fix the two straight straws to the cardboard, close to two opposite edges
With the help of an adult carefully use the scissors to make a small hole in the centre of each plastic lid.
Put one skewer through each straw and force the sharp ends into the perforated plastic lids to form 2 axles and 4 wheels.
Use the scissors to cut the bottom end of the bendy straw and keep the bendy part.
Secure the bendy straw to the mouth of a balloon using the rubber band.
Using the sticky tape, fix the bendy straw to the upper side of the cardboard. (The car is now complete, wheels on the ground and a limp balloon on the top.)
While holding the cardboard, blow air into the balloon through the straw. Don't release the air.
Place the car with its wheels on the ground and release the air.
What happens?
Try experimenting with changing the amount of air you put into your balloon, Does the car travel further?
Explanation: When you inflate the balloon, the stretched rubber stores potential energy. When you release the balloon, this potential energy is converted to kinetic energy as the car begins to move forward. The car will eventually stop but the energy is not lost - it has been converted to other forms of energy such as sound and heat.

3 - Action and Reaction

Aim: To demonstrate Newton's Third Law of Motion.

Materials Required

- 1 x pen
- 1 x ruler or measure tape
- 1 x pair of roller blades or roller skates
- 1 x large ball

Method

While wearing roller skates or rollerblades, stand straight and motionless on a hard level surface.
Hold the ball with both hands and throw it forward. What happens?
Measure the distance you travelled on your skates.
Now try throwing the ball with greater force.
Does the distance of travel change?
Explanation: When you throw the ball forward, you move backward. The harder you throw the ball the further both you and the ball travel.
Does Action/Reaction play a part in the previous two experiments?

4 - Film Canister Rocket

Aim: To demonstrate the principle of rocket travel.

Required Materials

- 1 x empty plastic canister and lid from 35mm film. (White canisters work better than black)
- 1 x Alka-Seltzer tablet or other fizzing antacid tablet (Get this from your parents)
- 2 x tablespoons of water (1 fluid ounce or 30ml)
- 1 x pair of Safety goggles

This experiment must be done outdoors, under adult supervision, and you must wear safety goggles.

Method

Go outside.
Put on the safety goggles.
Remove the lid from the film canister and pour the water into the canister.
Before moving to the next step, read the instructions to the end, and prepare yourself and your materials.
Break the antacid tablet in half.
Drop one half of the tablet half into the canister.
Snap on the cap of the canister (make sure that it snaps on tightly.)
Place the canister on the ground with the cap side down and step back at least 2 metres.
After 10-15 seconds, you will hear a "POP". What happens next?
If no POP is heard, wait at least 30 seconds before approaching the canister. (If the POP is lost, it is usually because the cap has not been fitted tightly and the gas has leaked out)
Explanation: When the tablet begins to dissolve, a gas (carbon dioxide) is released, creating pressure (potential energy) inside the film canister. As more gas is released, the pressure builds until the cap is thrust downwards (kinetic energy) and the canister rocket is thrust upwards.
In a real rocket the thrust is generated by burning fuel to create hot gases.

5 - Water Rockets

Aim: To demonstrate how pressure builds to create thrust. Consolidating the lesson of the film canister rocket.

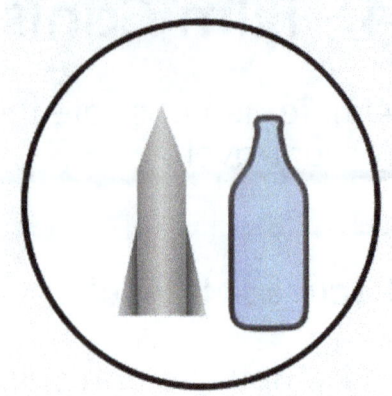

This experiment must be done outdoors, under adult supervision, and you must wear safety goggles.

Materials Required

- 1 x empty plastic bottle (approximately 1 Litre)
- 1 x cardboard circle cut and taped to form a cone to fit the bottom of the bottle.
- 4 x cardboard fins
- 1 x cork to fit the opening of the bottle
- An air pump with a needle adaptor
- Water

Method

Push the needle adaptor of the pump through the cork. (If the cork is too long for the needle, trim the cork in length.)
Attach the cone and four fins to the bottle. The cone goes on the bottom, and the fins around the opening.
Fill the bottle one quarter full of water and push in the cork tightly.
Take the bottle outside and connect the pump to the needle adaptor.
Stand the bottle upside down on a solid surface resting on the fins.
Ensure all spectators are standing well back.
Pump air into the bottle until something happens. What do you think will happen after you pump air into the bottle?
Do not approach the rocket once you have started pumping - even if it looks like nothing is happening.

6 - Egg Dropping

Aim: To teach children about momentum and how different materials can reduce momentum.

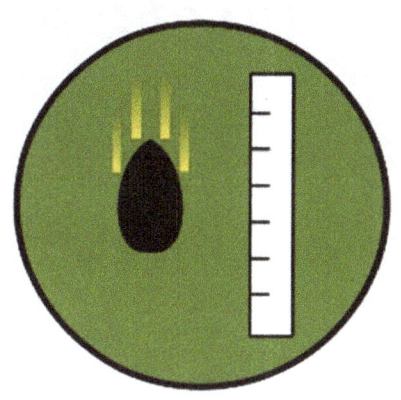

Materials Required

- Ziploc bags (as many as you want)
- Hard boiled eggs
(as many as your mother will allow you)
- Padding materials such as
- bubble wrap
- tissues
- rags
- paper sheets
- dry cereal
- facial tissues
- etc.
- 1 x ruler or measuring tape

Method

Fill a Ziploc bag with one type of padding material.
Put one egg inside the filled bag and seal it.
Repeat the process as many times as you want filling the Ziploc bags with different padding materials.
Drop each bag from the same height.
Make a note of the result – did the shell crack? How extensively?
If you have sufficient eggs, you can repeat the experiment using gradually greater heights.
Try to predict what will happen each time.

7 - Baking soda rocket

Aim: To further instill the lessons learned in Experiments 1, 4 & 5, - building pressure to generate thrust.

Materials Required:

- 1 x empty plastic bottle (approximately 500ml)
- 1 x cork suitable as a stopper for the bottle
- 3 x tablespoon (60 ml) baking soda (bicarbonate of soda)
- 3 x cups vinegar or lemon juice
- 3 x straight straws
- 1 x roll of sticky tape
- 1 x sheet of paper towel
- 1 pair of safety goggles

This experiment must be done outdoors, under adult supervision, and you must wear safety goggles.

Method:

1. Using sticky tape, fix the 3 straws to the bottle to make the "legs" for your rocket. The bottle opening should be facing down when the bottle is standing on its legs. Make sure the legs are placed high enough to allow for 1-2" of space between the bottle opening and the flat surface below.
2. Make sure the cork fits tightly in the bottle.
3. Remove the cork and turn the bottle over so that the pencil legs are facing up. Using a funnel, add 2-3 cups of vinegar or lemon juice to the bottle.
4. Take the square of paper towel. Place the baking soda onto the centre of the paper towel. Roll the paper towel tightly so that it will fit inside bottle opening. DO NOT place in the bottle.
5. Move the equipment to a level hard surface outside and put on the safety goggles.
6. Quickly place your paper towel packet inside the bottle and plug with cork.
7. Place the bottle on its "legs" and stand back.
What do you think will happen?
8. If nothing seems to be happening, DO NOT approach the rocket for at least 3 minutes.

8 - Self inflating balloon

Aim: To demonstrate how mixing baking soda and vinegar generates gas, like the mixing of chemical components to produce rocket fuel.

Materials Required:

- 1 x party balloon
- 1 x empty plastic bottle (approximately 1 Litre)
- 1 x funnel
- 1 teaspoon (5 ml) baking soda
- 3 tablespoons (60 ml) of vinegar

Method:

1. Using a funnel, add 1 teaspoon of baking soda to the bottle.
2. Using the funnel pour the vinegar into the balloon.
3. Holding the balloon by its neck, carefully stretch the open end of the balloon and place it over the mouth of the bottle, while leaving the rest of the balloon hanging.
4. Hold tightly to the balloon at the point where it is attached to the bottle. Lift the body of the balloon to pour the vinegar into the bottle, all the while holding the balloon at the mouth of the bottle.
5. When the vinegar interacts with the baking soda on the bottom of the bottle, carbon dioxide gas is generated and will inflate the balloon.
6. You can experiment by varying the amount of baking soda you place in the bottle – rinse the bottle well before placing more baking soda inside.

The Planets of Our Solar System

"**Mercury**: the closest planet to our Sun, at just 58 million kilometres (km) ... Despite its reputation for being sun-baked and molten, it is not the hottest planet in our Solar System ..."

"**Venus**: the second closest planet to our Sun, orbiting at an average distance of 108 million km ... it is often called Earth's "sister planet," as it is just a little smaller than Earth ... due to ... (the composition of) its atmosphere, which has a high concentration of greenhouse gases, and its proximity to the Sun, Venus is the Solar Systems hottest planet ..."

"**Earth**: Our home, and the only planet in our Solar System (that we know of) that actively supports life ..."

"**Mars**: the fourth planet from the sun, at a distance of about 228 million km ... It is also known as "the Red Planet" because of its reddish hue, which is due to the prevalence of iron oxide on its surface ..."

"**Jupiter**: Jupiter is the fifth planet from the Sun, at a distance of about 778 million km ... Jupiter is also the most massive planet in our Solar System, being 317 times the mass of Earth, and two and half times larger than all the other planets combined ..."

"**Saturn**: Saturn is the sixth planet from the Sun at a distance of about 1.4 billion km ... Saturn is most famous and most easily recognized for its spectacular ring system ..."

"**Uranus**: Uranus is the seventh planet from the sun at a distance of about 2.9 billion km ... The presence of methane ice is ... what gives it its bluish appearance ... Uranus is also the coldest planet in our Solar System ..."

"**Neptune:** Neptune is the eighth and farthest planet from the Sun, at a distance of about 4.5 billion km ..."

"**Pluto:** With much controversy ... Pluto was reclassified as a dwarf planet in 2006 ..."

Source of quotes: Order Of the Planets From The Sun - Universe Today (https://www.universetoday.com/72305/order-of-the-planets-from-the-sun/)

This Photo by Unknown Author is licensed under CC BY-SA

Jewish Education and Space Flight

By Velvl Greene

The Rebbe (Rabbi Menachem Mendel Schneerson, leader of the Lubavitch Hassidim, based in Brooklyn, New York), who was trained as an engineer, had a keen understanding of the physical world and how it worked. So when the Apollo spaceship landed on the moon in 1969, he used that scientific achievement to make a point about Jewish education.

In the NASA program, the Rebbe understood, there had always been a problem with balancing weight limits versus fuel needs in space flights. It's a conundrum: If you build a rocket that will go a long distance, you'll need to carry a lot of fuel. But the more fuel you carry, the larger the fuel container has to be—which means the weight of the spacecraft is increased. The heavier the spacecraft, the more fuel you need. It's an endless cycle, and a critical issue if your mission takes you beyond the local environment to the moon or Mars.

Engineers settled on a solution: They built multi-staged rockets that contained several individual fuel tanks. The largest amount of fuel is needed in the first minutes of the flight, as the rocket takes off from the ground. So the fuel for those first four or five minutes goes into a separate container, and when the fuel is used, the empty container is jettisoned off. When you watch a launch, you'll see it. After a few minutes, the used-up fuel container drops away.

The next stage of the flight uses up the next-most fuel, because the rocket is still fighting the gravity of the earth. When that fuel tank is empty, it's also jettisoned, as are several more stages. As each tank of fuel is used and the container jettisoned, the overall weight of the spacecraft becomes lighter, so it needs less fuel.

By the time you're weightless, out of the pull of Earth's gravity, you'll need only a tiny bit of fuel. Because there's no resistance to fight against, a thimbleful of fuel will propel the craft a very long distance.

So the Rebbe used this to explain a passage in Mishlei (Proverbs 22:6), that we are to "educate a young person according to his path." That phrase has always been problematical, the Rebbe said. What does it mean, "according to his path"?

It's very simple, the Rebbe said. It's something we do in education all the time. We introduce a three-year-old child to the aleph-bet (First and second letters of the Hebrew alphabet), and we make a big fuss about it. We have a party, we give him candy, we celebrate. In the old days, we'd even put honey on the page itself. The child sees the big fuss, he likes the candy, and he's very interested. He learns.

When the child gets to be about five years old, candy doesn't motivate him anymore. So we move to a different incentive, maybe toys or a tricycle.

Then when he's 10 or 11, toys don't work anymore. By that time, he wants electronic games. That's what we're doing—educating a child according to his path. We're using an incentive that's meaningful to him at his age level.

This, the Rebbe said, is exactly the same principle as that of the multistage rocket. That which is not needed any longer is jettisoned. We don't want to carry the extra weight along.

When you reach the next level of understanding and learning, you get rid of the weight, you don't need as much inspiration as before in order to push yourself. By the time you reach a certain stage of learning, all you need is just a tiny bit of fuel to propel you forward.

A former Fulbright scholar and pioneer in exobiology (the study of life beyond Earth), Professor Velvl Greene spent years working for NASA searching for life on Mars. He continued to lecture right up until his passing in 2011. This story is adapted from Curiosity and the Desire for Truth (Arthur Kurzweil Publishers, October 2015).

This article may also be read at: https://www.chabad.org/library/article_cdo/aid/3170865/jewish/Jewish-Education-and-Space-Flight.htm

This story was also retold by Mendel Kalmenson under the heading "Rocket Science" on pages 50-51 of his book Seeds of Wisdom, Jewish Educational Media, New York 2013

Contributors to this work

Chol, Tikvah Malkah, Illustrator
Donna the Astronomer (donnatheastronomer.com.au)
Greenwald, Miriam
Greenwald, Sarah
Skilton, Peter (Dr), President, Mornington Peninsula Astronomical Society
Stern, Harvey (Dr)

www.ingramcontent.com/pod-product-compliance
Lightning Source LLC
Chambersburg PA
CBHW060522010526
44107CB00060B/2659